True and Happy

Written and Illustrated by
Ron and Rebekah Coriell

A publication of
ASSOCIATION OF CHRISTIAN SCHOOLS INTERNATIONAL
P.O. BOX 4097, WHITTIER, CA 90607

Copyright © 1985 by Association of Christian Schools International. Adapted by permission from materials formerly copyrighted by Christian School Curriculum, a division of Fleming H. Revell Company. All rights reserved. Printed in the United States of America. This publication, or parts thereof, may not be reproduced in any form by photographic, electrostatic, mechanical, or any other method, for any use, including information storage and retrieval, without written permission from the publisher.

Honesty
tree

Truthful Words and Ways

Wherefore putting away lying,
speak every man truth with
his neighbour....
                    Ephesians 4:25

Honesty in the Bible

The truth is not always popular. The Prophet Micaiah experienced this during the reign of King Ahab of Israel.

Jehoshaphat, king of Judah, and King Ahab decided to join forces and make war against the Syrians. To see if God would bless this venture, Jehoshaphat asked Ahab to check first with the Lord. Ahab called four hundred of his prophets together. These men were supposed to speak words from God. But God was not speaking through these men because of their wickedness. Nevertheless, they told the two kings to go to battle because God would help them to win.

To be on the safe side, the kings decided to check with one more prophet, Micaiah. Wicked Ahab hated this man of God. He always told Ahab things he didn't want to hear from God. Reluctantly, Ahab consulted him.

At first, Micaiah told the king to go to battle. But the king knew that the prophet did not mean what he said. So Ahab insisted that he tell him the truth. So Micaiah did, even though it was not popular. He said that he saw Ahab's army scattered over the hills after the battle with no leader, meaning that God would cause wicked Ahab to die in combat.

Turning to Jehoshaphat, Ahab said, "Didn't I tell you he never gives any good news about me?"

Ahab commanded that the prophet be put into jail and fed with bread and water. Then Ahab and Jehoshaphat went out to battle with the Syrians.

Everything happened just as Micaiah had said it would. Ahab was killed and his army defeated. God was pleased with His honest prophet.

This story is found in 1 Kings 22:8-37; 2 Chronicles 18:1-34.

Honesty of a Hero of the Faith

"It's not worth the money," complained the customer.

"I beg your pardon, sir," said Henry, the store clerk. "Upon my word, this piece of leather is superior in native quality and workmanship. It's worth every penny of the price we are asking. Isn't that so?" asked Henry, turning to the other apprentices for support.

All his fellow workers except one heartily agreed that the leather piece was worth the price asked. But young William Bramwell remained silent at his bench. He knew that Henry was lying.

Then, standing, he said loudly and clearly, "No, sir, the quality of that leather is not as good as you say it is. The customer is right and he should not have to pay that much."

The workers looked at each other in disbelief. William was blocking a sale. What would Mr. Brandreth, the owner, say when he found out?

Suddenly the owner appeared at the doorway between the shop and his living quarters.

Addressing the customer he said, "Yes, you're right, sir. William has told you the truth. The leather is not top quality. You may have it for ten percent off the price."

With a grateful look at William, the customer bought the leather and left.

"William," began Mr. Brandreth, "your truthful words and ways are a good example to the rest of your fellow workers."

It sometimes takes courage to be completely honest, but God always honors those who are honest.

William Bramwell's honesty in his youth prepared him to be used by God as a great preacher. He later won thousands to Christ in England in the early 1800s.

Honesty at Home

"Mom, I just can't share my bedroom with Timmy!" exclaimed Richard.

"My, you seem pretty serious about that," answered Mother with a surprised look. "What's the problem?"

"Timmy is messy. He's forgetful. He's careless. And he does not care how our room looks. I try to do my part. I make my bed faithfully. I pick up my clothes. Why, I even do some of his cleanup work. But his half of the room is always sloppy."

Richard paused to catch his breath long enough for Mother to give some advice.

"Have you ever told your brother how you feel?" she asked. "When two Christians have a disagreement, they should talk it out first with each other. That's what the Bible says in Matthew 18."

"I know, Mother, but you don't understand," responded Richard. "Timmy is so sensitive. He cries at the least little thing. I don't want to hurt his feelings."

"Oh, I understand, Richard," replied Mother. "But it will be worse if you don't tell him the truth in a kind way. Be honest with him. The Bible says to speak the truth in love."

Mother wasn't sure Richard would heed her counsel, but he did. Surprisingly, Timmy did not cry or become angry with Richard. Because he loved his older brother, Timmy wanted to please him. In no time at all, Timmy's side of the room was kept as clean as Richard's. Richard was glad he was honest in a loving way.

Honesty at School

Richard grew nervous as his teacher began the spelling test. His father had promised a camping trip if he received an *A* in spelling.

The first nine words were easy and Richard began to feel confident. Then his teacher gave the final word. Richard's mind went blank. He just could not remember how the word was spelled. Lightly, in pencil on the back of the paper, he tried writing the word two different ways, but neither looked correct.

"Now what will I do?" thought Richard.

He could hear each tick of the clock. Time was running out. If he moved in his seat just a little, he might be able to see Marlene's paper. She was the best speller in the class. Richard was really tempted, but a Bible verse he had learned in Sunday school helped him to do right. "The eyes of the Lord are in every place, beholding the evil and the good" (Proverbs 15:3). He knew God would see him if he were dishonest. That would be sin and make Jesus sad. Richard turned his paper in, knowing he had only spelled nine words correctly.

That grading period Richard received a *B* in spelling. He thought he would never get to go camping. He told his father about his temptation to cheat. To his surprise, Father was so happy about his truthful ways that he promised to take him camping anyway. Richard was glad that he had acted honestly.

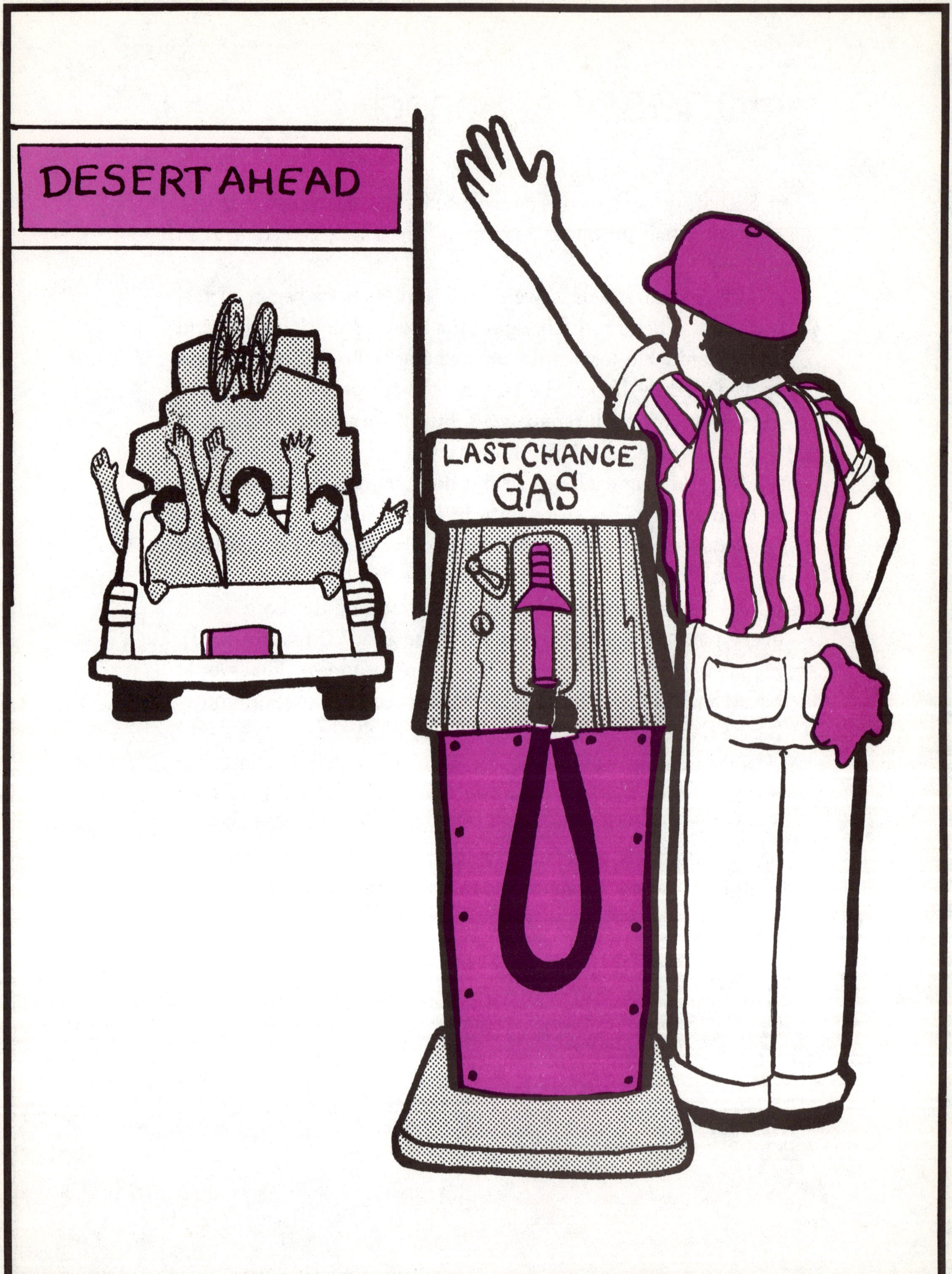
DESERT AHEAD
LAST CHANCE
GAS

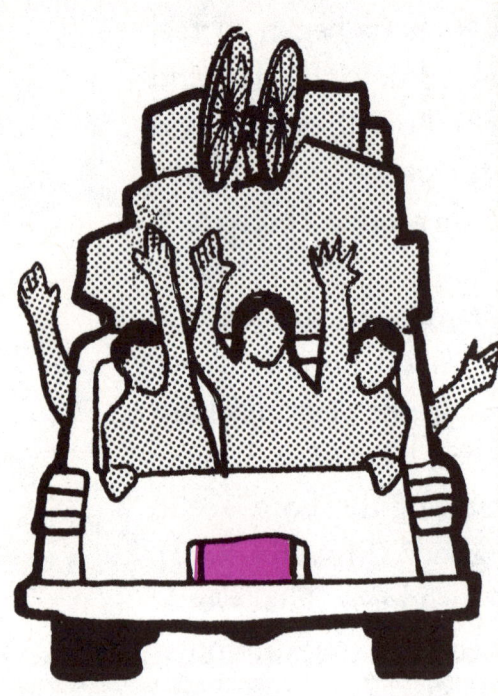

Thankful

tankful

Being Grateful and Saying So

In every thing give thanks: for this is the will of God in Christ Jesus concerning you.
                    1 Thessalonians 5:18

Thankfulness in the Bible

Ten men huddled together on the street. No one would come near them. Their clothes were tattered and torn. Sores and scabs covered their bodies and only patches of hair remained on their heads. Being considered unclean, they were not allowed to live near healthy people. They even had to warn people of their coming by shouting out, "Unclean, unclean!" These ten men had the dreaded disease called leprosy.

As Jesus entered the village where these sick men lived, many people ran to Him to seek His help. But the ten lepers could not go near the crowd. So they cried out in a loud voice, "Master, have mercy on us!"

Jesus was touched by their plight and commanded them to go and show themselves unto the priests at the synagogue.

As the men turned and went, they noticed that their skin was free of sores and scabs. They were healed! The leprosy was gone!

One of the men stopped, turned back, and ran to Jesus. With a loud voice he praised and glorified God.

Jesus was happy with this man's thankfulness. He saw how grateful the leper was because he had come back to say so.

This story is found in Luke 17:11-19.

Thankfulness
of a Hero of the Faith

"Children, get up quickly!" shouted Samuel Wesley. "Don't bother to get dressed. Just get outside as fast as you can! The house is on fire!"

Flames burst onto the roof of the house. The darkness of the midnight hour was lighted by the fire. Older brothers grabbed the hands of their sisters. Reverend Wesley directed his large family out the door and to a safe spot some distance away.

No fire department would be able to save the building from destruction on this night in 1709. The Wesleys helplessly watched as their beloved home burned to the ground. Both sorrow and thankfulness filled the hearts of this godly family. As father Wesley led them in a prayer of thanksgiving, he thanked God for His perfect will and for the safety of everyone.

Suddenly, above the crackle and cracking of burning embers, came the sounds of a child's screams. Instantly, Reverend Wesley recognized the voice.

"Young John is still in the house!" he shouted fearfully.

Before Mrs. Wesley could utter a quick "Be careful," Reverend Wesley rushed back to the flaming fire to rescue his son. The doorway was aflame, forcing Samuel Wesley to climb upon a man's shoulders to reach where John was calling from. He was snatched from the clutches of a fiery death, seconds before the burning, thatched roof fell in.

John Wesley always felt that this rescue was a direct intervention of God. A second thanksgiving prayer was offered that night. This time *everyone* was present.

Thankfulness at Home

"Mother, I just don't understand," said Philip. "How can I be thankful that Father is in the hospital?"

Mrs. Hall replied, "We must be thankful because the Bible says, 'In every thing give thanks . . . .'" (1 Thessalonians 5:18).

"But I just don't feel thankful," protested Philip.

"I know you don't," replied Mother. "I miss your father as much as you do. To be thankful means to be grateful and to say so. Even though we don't feel like it, let's just tell God thank you, all right?"

"All right, Mother," answered Philip. "I'll try."

They bowed their heads and prayed.

"Dear Lord," said Philip. "I don't know why Dad is sick now. I wish he were home. But I will thank You now, even though I don't feel thankful."

Mother added, "And thank You, Lord, for being in control. All things will work out for good to those who love the Lord. We say, thank You. In Jesus' name, amen."

A few weeks later, Father was able to come home from the hospital. Philip and Mother were so glad.

"I'm really thankful that the Lord put me in the hospital," Father said.

Surprised, Philip replied, "Why is that?"

"Because I was able to be a witness to my roommate and lead him to the Lord," answered Father.

A real joy entered Philip's heart. Now, he was thankful that Father had been in the hospital. He could not only be grateful and say it but now he could feel it, too.

Thankfulness at School

"Oh, come on, Philip, you can't be serious!" shouted his friends in chorus.

"Thank Mr. Bloom?" questioned another. "He was the hardest teacher we had all year. I was fortunate to get a *D*."

"Don't bother to thank him," said another. "Just be thankful that this class is over."

Philip didn't know how to respond to his friends. As they walked away laughing at the thought of being grateful to their science teacher, he just shook his head.

"The Bible says, 'In every thing give thanks . . . .'" (1 Thessalonians 5:18) thought Philip. "I'm just thankful to God that I earned a *C*. I really had to work hard for it. But I also appreciate Mr. Bloom's teaching. He knew his science and how to make class interesting. He was always willing to take time in class to answer my questions. One day, he even spent an hour after school explaining how a plant grows by taking in water, minerals, and sunlight."

Philip turned around and weaved his way back into the school building as students were streaming out, report cards in their hands. He found Mr. Bloom in the science lab sitting at his desk.

"Excuse me," Philip said softly. "I just wanted to say thank you for being such a good teacher. I know I only received a *C*, but I learned a lot."

Mr. Bloom's face broke into a warm smile. "You are welcome, Philip. You have really made my day happy. I sometimes wonder if it's worth it all to try so hard as I teach my classes. But now I can see it is indeed worth it. Thank you for being grateful and saying so."

Joy
ahoy

Being Happy Inside and Out

And my soul shall be joyful in the Lord: it shall rejoice in his salvation.

Psalms 35:9

Joyfulness in the Bible

The crowd of people buzzed with excitement as Peter and the apostles taught about Jesus and healed the sick. But also among the throng were those who hated these men and their Gospel. They were the Sanhedrin, the religious rulers of Israel.

They had warned the apostles not to preach Christ and even had thrown them in jail. But God sent an angel by night to open the doors and rescue them. By dawn's light, they were once again in the streets telling others about the resurrected Saviour.

Upon hearing that the escapees were once more preaching, police were sent out to arrest them again. They were careful not to do it violently, for they feared the people would kill them.

Standing before the Sanhedrin once again, the apostles were firmly rebuked.

"Did not we strictly command you that ye should not teach in this name? and, behold, ye have filled Jerusalem with your doctrine, and intend to bring this man's blood upon us" (Acts 5:28).

They would have killed the apostles right there if it were not for the intercession of a wise council member. He advised the Sanhedrin to wait and see if God blessed or rejected the work of these preachers.

So the apostles were spared death at this time. But they were not let go until they had been soundly beaten for disobeying these jealous religious rulers.

How sad and discouraged most people would be after so difficult a trial. But they loved Jesus so much that they were willing to suffer pain joyfully to preach about their Lord.

This story is found in Acts 5:16-42.

Joyfulness
of a Hero of the Faith

What made Jonathan Goforth happy was telling people about Jesus Christ. When this Canadian was saved in 1877, he became a missionary at home. He joyfully started passing out tracts Sunday after Sunday at his church.

Later, while in Bible school, Jonathan was asked to speak at a church some distance away. But he only had enough money in his pocket to buy a ticket that could get him part of the way there. He would have to leave the train at a station ten miles short of his destination. Most people would have been discouraged, but not Jonathan. His greatest joy was to speak to people about his Lord. He wasn't going to let a ten-mile walk stop him.

He bought a ticket and rode to the last station. Then he began to walk the remaining miles. When he had traveled about eight miles, he came upon a group of men repairing the road. He stopped to witness to them and invite them to the church services. He was not sure if they would come, but at least he had the joy of presenting the Gospel to them. On Sunday, to his surprise, several of the men attended. And, to his greater joy, one of them accepted Christ as his Saviour.

Goforth later commented, "I would gladly walk ten miles any day to bring one lost soul to Christ."

A joyful spirit helped Jonathan to walk those long miles and be a witness. God was pleased and later used him to be a great missionary to China.

Joyfulness at Home

"Mom, come quickly. I've got red spots all over my face and neck," cried Martha.

Coming into the room, Mother suspected what the problem was. As she looked at Martha closely, she shook her head.

"You have the measles," she announced. "You'll have to stay inside until you are well."

"No, not that," pleaded Martha. "My friends and I had special plans for today. Do I have to, Mom?"

"Yes, you'll just have to make the best of it and try to be joyful," replied Mother.

Martha didn't want to face the fact. "How can I be happy and stay in all weekend? What a boring way to spend Saturday and Sunday." But to her surprise, it turned out to be one of the most interesting and joyful weekends that she had ever spent indoors.

Saturday morning she heard that an elderly Christian lady in the church had fallen and hurt her hip. Not having anything better to do, she asked her mother if she could telephone her and tell her that she was praying for her. What started out to be a short talk ended up lasting one hour. The lady was so thrilled at Martha's call that she talked on and on and on. Martha's spirit of sadness over her measles changed to joy as she sensed how happy the lady felt talking with her.

When Martha hung up the telephone, she felt happy. If she hadn't become sick, she probably wouldn't have called the elderly lady. Then she would have missed the blessing of making someone feel joyful.

Joyfulness at School

Martha sat looking sadly out the classroom window. The sun was shining and the birds were singing. But she was not enjoying any of it. Before she could go outside for recess, she had to complete her assignment.

"Work, work, work," she thought. "That's all I do. I thought that students were supposed to have some fun at school. That's what would make me happy."

"What's the matter?" questioned the teacher.

Martha replied, "How can anybody be joyful about working?"

Sitting on a stool beside Martha, the teacher said, "I think joyfulness must be something you learn to do as you build good habits while you're young. That's one reason children go to school and have assignments to do."

"But it is hard to be joyful when I see all this work," responded Martha.

The teacher pointed outside to the big oak tree. "See those birds singing? They appear to be quite happy. Yet, all day long they work to find food and keep the nest clean. I'm glad God made them joyful in their work or we would never hear their happy chirping. Perhaps our bird friends can be a helpful reminder that it pleases the Lord Jesus to see us joyful in our work."

Martha's glum look began to disappear. The teacher's encouraging words had helped to change her spirit.

"All right," she said, "I'll try to be joyful like the birds. Would you help me with this math?"

"Sure I will, Martha," said the teacher with a grin. "I am sure that your new spirit will make working a joy."

Character Development Challenges

This page is designed to give parents and teachers practical suggestions for teaching character traits to children.

Honesty

1. Help the student to discover the benefits of honesty in the following Bible verses: Proverbs 3:3; 16:6; Psalms 40:11; Proverbs 12:19; Psalms 43:3.
2. Proverbs 22:20, 21 state that the Book of Proverbs was written to acquaint us with truth. Each day the student should read a chapter from Proverbs and find one new thought of truth or advice.
3. To prevent lying, one should learn to control the tongue. Find steps to controlling the tongue in these verses: Psalms 39:1; Proverbs 4:24-27; 10:19; 14:23; Matthew 12:36; Proverbs 18:6; Ephesians 4:29; 5:4; Colossians 4:6.

Thankfulness

1. Have each student begin a "Thankful List." Each day he writes down an item that he is thankful for and states why he is thankful.
2. The student should find out what the Bible says he is to be thankful for. Read Psalms 26:7; Ephesians 5:20; 1 Timothy 2:1; 1 Thessalonians 5:18; Colossians 3:17.
3. Read Psalm 136. Then have each student create his own psalm, using the form of Psalm 136.

    I will thank the Lord for _____ because His mercy endureth forever.
    I will thank the Lord for _____ because His mercy endureth forever.
Write ten verses.

Joy

1. Read Matthew 5:3-12 and help each student to learn whom the Lord says are blessed or happy people.
2. Help the student discover what the Bible says brings joy. Read Proverbs 21:15; Psalms 16:11; 51:12; Isaiah 29:19; Jeremiah 15:16.
3. Read James 1:2. The student should recall a problem in his life and discover how God used that problem for good in his life. Then he can begin to rejoice that it happened.